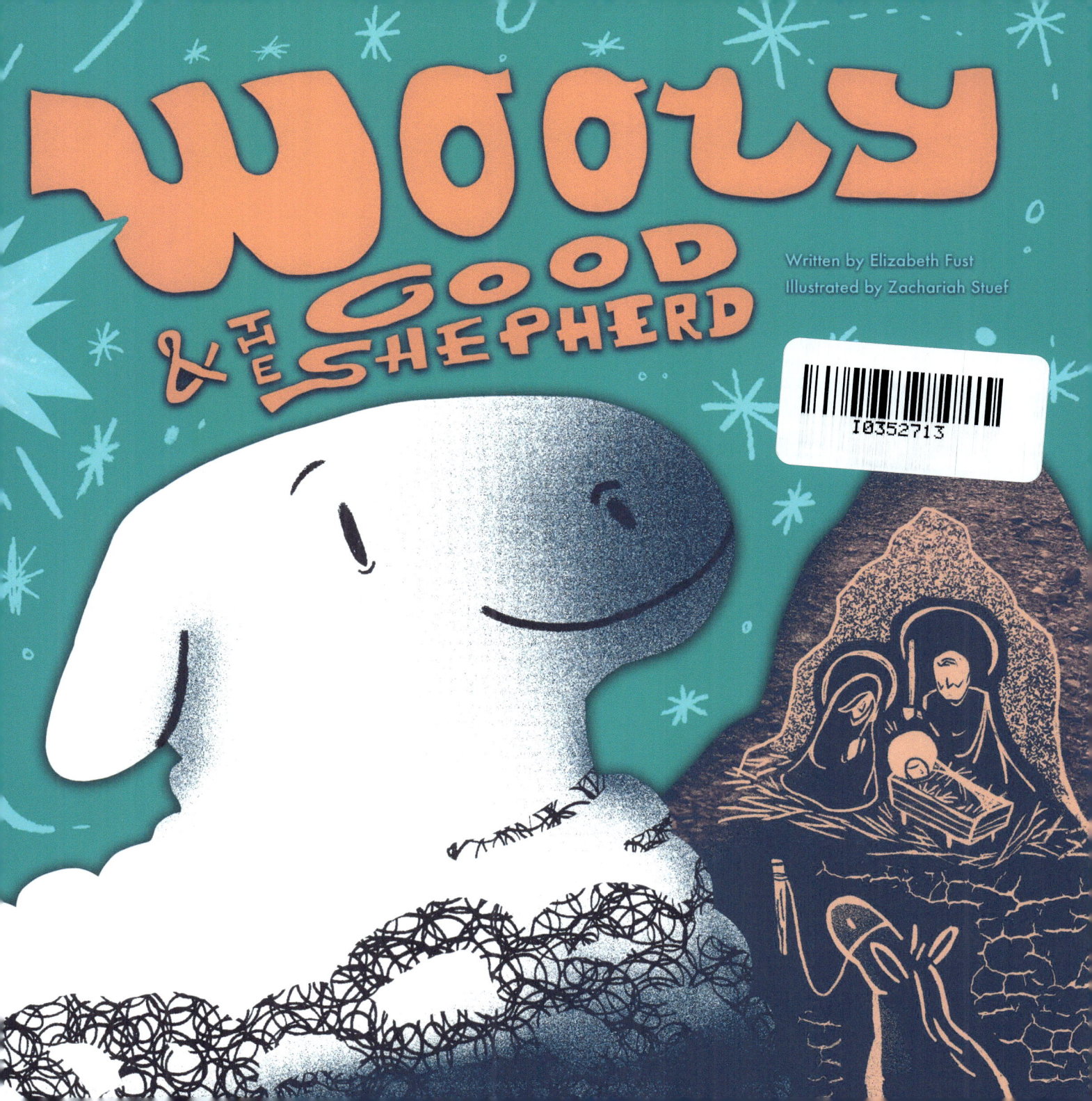

Wooly & The Good Shepherd

Copyright © 2020 Elizabeth Fust

No part of this work may be reproduced in any form or by any electronic or mechanical means, including information storage and retrieval systems, without written permission in writing from the author, except brief quotations for review purposes.

Editing by Jansina of Rivershore Books
Illustrations and book design by Zachariah Stuef

ISBN: 978-1-63522-018-6

Printed in the United States of America
10   9   8   7   6   5   4   3   2

Rivershore Books
8982 Van Buren St. NE · Minneapolis, MN 55434
763-670-8677 · info@rivershorebooks.com

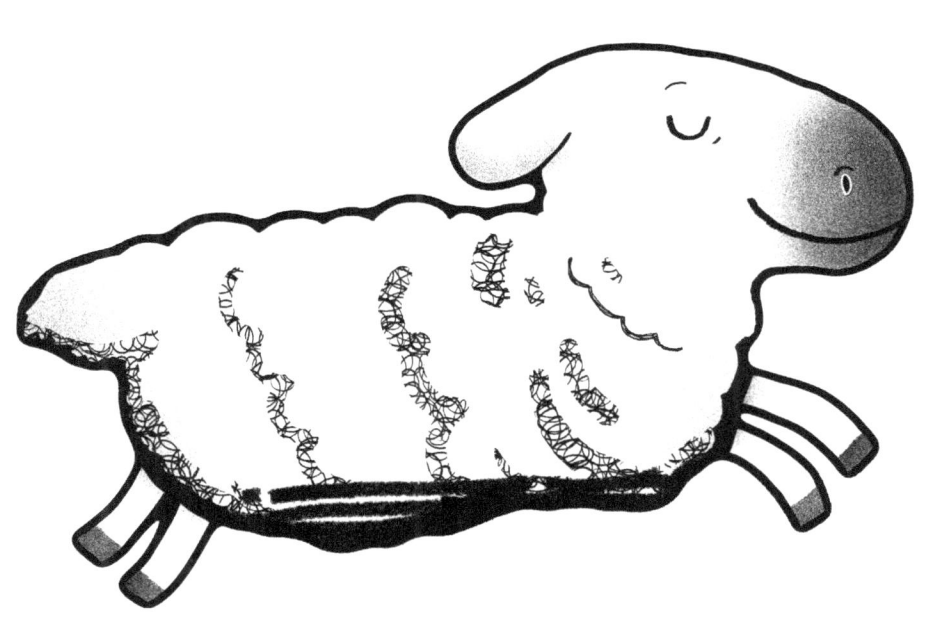

Wooly was a scaredy cat—only he was a little lamb, not a cat. He was having a bad day.
All day, crowds of people had been traveling past his pasture on their way to Bethlehem.
Wooly didn't like crowds; people scared him.
He was just a small little lamb, and humans were so big.
The only human Wooly liked was his Shepherd.

Wooly didn't know why so many people were coming to Bethlehem that day.

He only knew that it had something to do with the king.

All of the other sheep in the flock made fun of Wooly because he was scared of humans. And he was scared of bumblebees. And he was scared of wolves. And Wooly was even scared of the dark.

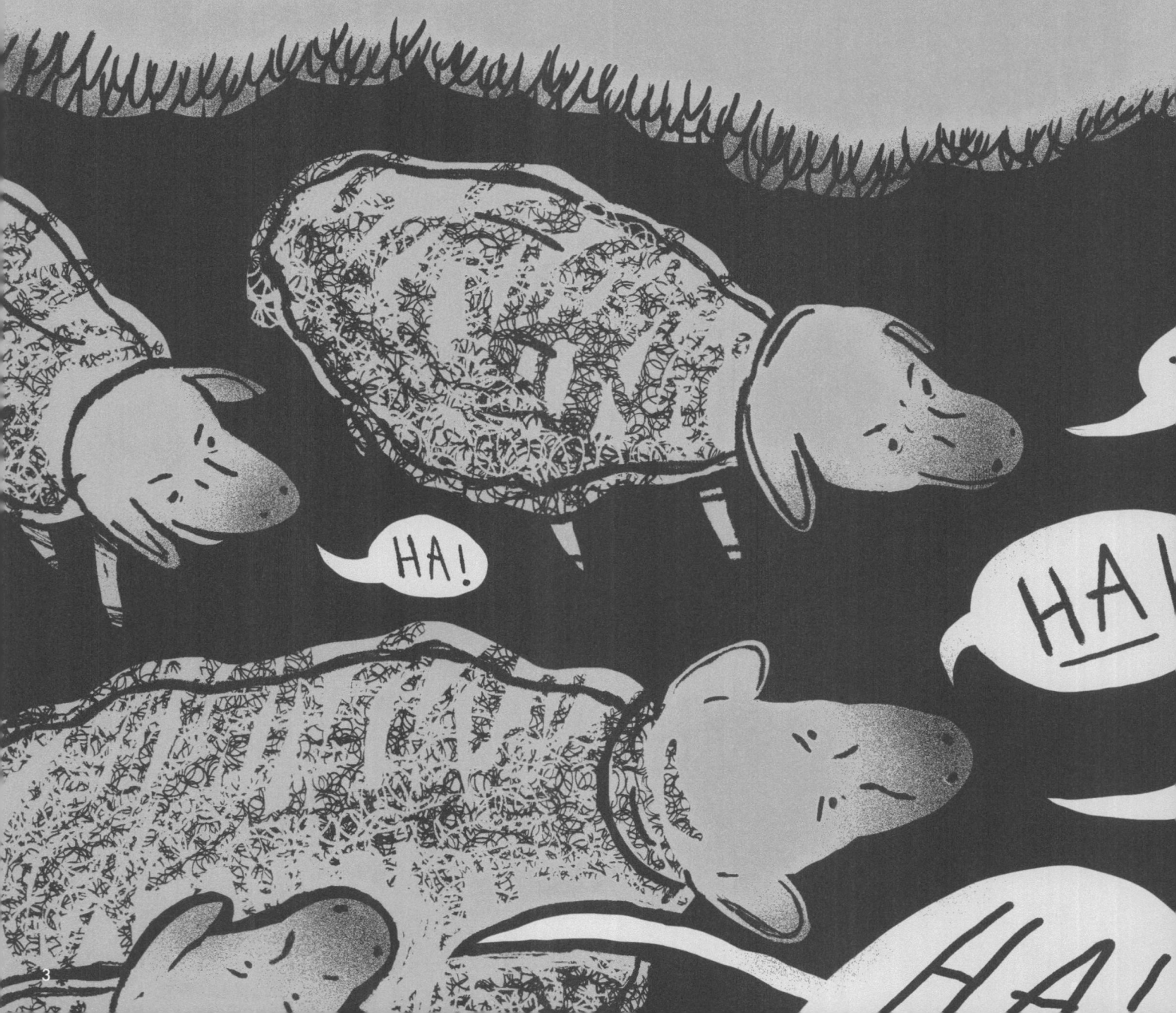

When the sun set, some of the other sheep laughed at Wooly and tried to frighten him with scary stories. "Leave Wooly alone," Wooly's kind Shepherd said, and they wandered off to find a comfy spot in the flock to fall asleep.

Wooly didn't go with the others to lie down in the pasture.
His Shepherd slept in the gateway of the pen to protect the sheep overnight
so Wooly curled up next to him. He was never afraid of scary things when his Shepherd was there.

Suddenly, in the middle of the night, the Shepherd got up, waking Wooly.
All the shepherds were looking at the sky.
A beautiful star lit up the nighttime so that the night wasn't even dark at all.

Something appeared in the sky. It was like a person, but with bird wings! Wooly hid behind his Shepherd. Then the birdperson spoke, "Do not be afraid." But Wooly was afraid of this strange birdperson!

"I come with news of great joy! Today in Bethlehem a child was born. You will find the infant wrapped in swaddling clothes and lying in a manger."

That doesn't make sense, Wooly thought. Mangers weren't for babies to sleep in, they were where the animals ate.

Then suddenly more birdpeople appeared. They filled the entire sky and started singing

"Glory to the newborn King! Peace on earth, and mercy mild, God and sinners reconciled! Christ is born in Bethlehem."

Wooly peeked out from behind his Shepherd. What did they mean, a newborn baby king? Shaking, Wooly stepped out from his hiding place to see the birdpeople.
"Look at all the angels, Wooly," his Shepherd said.
The birdpeople were called angels!

"They want us to go and follow that star," said the Shepherd.

All the shepherds woke up the flock
and started herding them along to follow the star.

"Where are we going? What's going on?" all the lambs were asking.
"Didn't you see all the angels?" Wooly asked.

But none of the lambs had, and they didn't believe Wooly when he told them the story.

The shepherds walked all the way to Bethlehem, where all the people had been going. There were so many people, one shepherd said, that the inns were all full and there were no more rooms left for anyone to stay! Wooly was glad the people were sleeping and not out on the road with the shepherds and sheep.

The shepherds finally stopped at a stable that was filled with many animals.
Inside, there was also a gentle-looking man and lady.
Wooly's Shepherd went to speak to them, leaving the sheep outside.
Then he called for all the other shepherds to look inside the manger.
Whatever the shepherds saw made them very excited.

"What's in there?"
one of the lambs asked.

"I don't know; you look!" another said. All the sheep were too scared.

"I'll go look!" Wooly said.
"No, Wooly, you won't look.
You're too scared!" all the lambs said.

Wooly had been the only lamb to see the angels.
He wanted to know what their song had meant.
He didn't want to be scared.
He was too curious; he wanted to be brave
and discover what was happening.
Slowly, Wooly started toward the manger.
What had made the shepherds so excited?
Usually mangers were used for food.
Maybe there was something good to eat.

He peeked his head into the manger, and then he saw it.
A baby! A happy little human baby.
The angels had said there was a newborn baby.
A newborn king!
Wooly nuzzled the baby with his nose,
and the baby laughed. Wooly liked the baby.
He wasn't scared of the baby human like he was
of big people. The baby reached out and touched
Wooly's nose. Wooly felt like he did with his Shepherd;
he was no longer scared.

"Come look; come see!" Wooly called to the other sheep.

"It's a baby — a baby king!"

All the sheep and shepherds crowded in; there were lots of smiles and laughter and baaing. Because Wooly had been brave, he had gotten to meet the baby king.

The angels had said there would be peace on earth.
After meeting the baby king, Wooly felt at peace.
Wooly felt like he did with his Shepherd.
Wooly wasn't afraid of anything anymore.

Elizabeth Fust
(Author)

Elizabeth has been writing since she was a little girl and plans to still be writing when she is a little old lady. Elizabeth is the author of this picture book and The Hungry Kitten's Tale picture book. She has also written many short stories and feature articles about her adventures. Elizabeth's writing is greatly inspired by the beauty surrounding her home where she lives between Lake Superior and the mountains of Michigan's Upper Peninsula.

Facebook and Instagram: Elizabeth Fust Books
Website: https://elizabethfust.wixsite.com/
            booksbyelizabethfust

Zachariah Stuef
(Illustrator)

Zachariah has always wanted to illustrate articles, books, and advertisements. He feels honored to have "Wooly" as his first illustrated kid's book job. Most, if not all, of Zachariah's work is inspired by his faith, overactive imagination, and the latin phrase "Carpe Diem!" In the past he has illustrated for Our Daily Bread Ministries, Unleash The Gospel Detroit, & Passages North.

Instagram: @stuefcreative
Other social media: Stuef Creative
Website: https://www.stuefcreative.com

Dedicated to my mom and dad. Thank you for helping me dream, write, and publish.

A special thank you to the Meister family and Meister's Christmas Tree Farm for your friendship and support.

Acknowledgments

Thank you Zach for your hard work and creativity! You brought my story to life better than I could have imagined.

Thank you Jansina of Rivershore Books for your great work! Your help, friendship, and mentorship mean so much to me.

Thank you Katelyn Meister, Elizabeth Bertucci, Amy Jo Klas, and everyone who beta-read Wooly and the Good Shepherd!

Rivershore Books

www.rivershorebooks.com
info@rivershorebooks.com

www.ingramcontent.com/pod-product-compliance
Lightning Source LLC
Chambersburg PA
CBHW041108070526
44583CB00002B/114